ROOTS AND VALUES IN CANADIAN LIVES

This attractive little volume which represents a reshaping of the Plaunt Lectures delivered at Carleton University, 1960, presents reflections on the art of living in Canada by one who has been deeply concerned with the relationships between our two cultures. The author examines the reflections of these cultures in its two literatures, describes his own personal experience of living with members of both groups, and goes on to analyse what contribution Canadian universities might make to greater understanding of our biculturalism. Canada, says the author, is not a datum but a construct; it is a becoming. Patterns and objectives have to be constantly redefined and improvised, with both parties in our dualism collaborating to create a well-tempered, yet positive, national life.

JEAN-C. FALARDEAU was born in Quebec City; studied at Sainte-Marie and Brébeuf Colleges in Montreal; at Laval in Quebec and the University of Chicago. A Fellow of the Royal Society of Canada, he was a member of the Canadian delegation to the Ninth General Conference of UNESCO, 1956, has been chairman of the Canadian Social Science Research Council, and of the Quebec branch of the Canadian Institute of International Affairs. He is now chairman of the department of sociology in the Faculté des Sciences Sociales, Université Laval, and joint editor of the quarterly *Recherches sociographiques;* he publishes and lectures widely on topics relating to the social life and artistic activities of Quebec and of Canada as a whole.

Alan B. Plaunt Memorial Lectures
Carleton University, Ottawa, March 24, 26, 1960

ROOTS AND VALUES IN CANADIAN LIVES

Jean-C. Falardeau

Published
in co-operation with Carleton University
by University of Toronto Press

ALAN B. PLAUNT MEMORIAL LECTURES

Canada and its Giant Neighbour. By Jacob Viner (1958)

Civil Liberties and Canadian Federalism.
By F. R. Scott (1959)

Roots and Values in Canadian Lives.
By Jean-C. Falardeau (1960)

University of Toronto Press

Diamond Anniversary 1961

BY WAY OF FOREWORD

I N March 1960 I was invited to give the Plaunt Memorial Lectures at Carleton University in Ottawa. Later, friendly pressures tried to convince me that these two talks should be published in book form. For better or for worse, I eventually acquiesced. Indeed, the basis of a tradition had been established, since the addresses of my two predecessors as Plaunt Lecturers, Professors Jacob Viner and Frank Scott, were already in print. Here, then, is my score for the Plaunt-Carleton third concerto.

I conceived my Plaunt lectures as an occasion for meditating on certain questions which have been crucial in my professional life and in my experience as a Canadian. The following pages do not offer a didactic essay in any sense of the term. They merely present reflections, often disconnected, which have sprung from personal observation, from sociological curiosity, from discussion with friends, here and there, over the years. They express the attitudes and the queries of one who was born and has lived in French Canada. The image of Canada which I carry within myself is shaped by this perspective. This image has been intermittently checked and transformed through constant communication with my French-Canadian compatriots, through dialogue with non-French transcontinental friends, through an effort towards grasping the whole of a country which still seems a mental construct. I offer it as I bear it, with the hope that it may serve as a reagent for more penetrating thoughts. And so,

> "The time has come," the Walrus said,
> "To talk of many things:
> Of shoes—and ships—and sealing-wax—
> Of cabbages—and kings—"
> Of TCA—and universities—
> Of our culture—and our gropings—
> Of those boring and friendly things
> That make us feel like Canadians. . . .

J.-C. F.

CONTENTS

ROOTS AND VALUES IN CANADIAN LIVES

I. OUR NEIGHBOUR'S
LIKENESS

I shall not be the first to begin a meditation on Canadian life by referring to its similarities with American life. The first phase in describing our countenance is to ascertain how much it looks like that of our neighbour. We in Canada are a mirror of others. The manner in which our houses are built, the ways in which people dress, eat, take their leisure, from Halifax to Vancouver, including Quebec and Montreal, do not differ greatly from those which are observed in Vermont, in Michigan, or on the Pacific seaboard. Restaurants, movie houses, office buildings, are interchangeable between Toronto and Rochester. So could be, in many instances, their occupants. Our daily routine of life, our domestic habits, our personality types have been patterned according to prototypes invented in the strangely brave new world south of our non-existent frontier. The heroes of youth and the myths of their parents have been transmitted to us from the south by the "verbivocovisual" media of mass communication. Suburbia also circumscribes our living space and our mental landscape. Our economic, administrative, civic, and religious institutions are run by organization men. For a great proportion, perhaps the majority of the families in our country as in the other, the ownership of a house, two cars, and a television set, represents the fulfilment of a life's ambition.

One peculiar paradox of the North American civilization, oriented as it is towards high productivity, is that the individual has been reduced, as Eric Fromm has pointed out, to the role of a consumer. He is a consumer not only of material goods which are offered to and imposed on him in greater and greater quantity, from soap suds to monstrous cars, but of all that was formerly reputed to be of an essentially personal character: how to spend his leisure time, how to behave with friends, how to think, how to pray. The individual in our society is no longer an active but a passive being. He is lived more than he lives. David Riesman has described him as an "other-directed" person. Social conformism has become his secular gospel of behaviour. The statistical average has been raised to the dignity of a moral norm. He values what is valued by his peers in the socio-economic stratum to which he belongs or to which he has the ambition to belong.

I choose an illustration of these modern mores from one of the few scientific accounts of Canadian social life. A sociological monograph entitled *Crestwood Heights*, published a few years ago, describes the relationships between parents, children, and the schools in an upper middle-class Canadian metropolitan suburb.[1] This is a social environment of superficial glamour and mechanized rusticity where the attitudes, the ideals, the social pressures are those made familiar to us through the cartoons of the *New Yorker*. The local sub-culture is heavily permeated by the North American dream, "a dream of a material heaven in the here and now, to be entered by the successful elect" (p. 6). This dream of material abundance is thought "to be achieved and maintained only by

[1]*Crestwood Heights*, by John R. Seeley, R. Alexander Sim, and Elizabeth Loosley (Toronto: University of Toronto Press, 1956).

unremitting struggle and constant sacrifice" (p. 6). Happiness "appears to be a blend of material well-being, success, social status, good physical and mental health" (p. 218). "A man is judged largely by the number and the quality of the things he owns." Accordingly, "the community serves the psychological purpose of a super-marketplace, where status may be validated in the acquisition and exhibition of material and non-material 'objects': houses, cars, clothes, jewellery, gadgets, furniture, works of art, stocks, bonds, membership in exclusive clubs, attendance at private schools" (p. 7).

The schools are the centre of the community, both in the physical and in the moral sense. Not only do they overshadow the various local churches but they have become the secular substitute for the church. The educational system and progressive educational theories are the *ersatz* form of religion. The key concepts of this educative process are those of adjustment and direct experience. The parents' ambition is to adapt themselves to their children, who are themselves in the process of becoming "adapted." They question themselves, they search their souls, because they feel that their children are spoiled, removed too far from reality. All they can do is to rely on advisers, on consultants, whom they find in the school system itself. "In Crestwood Heights, while the children are direct clients of the school, the parents have now become the indirect ones; in some cases they are equally dependent with their children on the school system" (p. 284). The process of socialization of the child and of the re-socialization of parents is polarized by social norms which are ends in themselves and devoid of any ethical content. The lay priests of this new religion are the mental health practitioners and the psychiatrists for whom Freud is God and Fromm his prophet. As the authors themselves put it: "The mental health practitioners—both therapists and educators—are, in effect, discharging priestly functions without the social structure of a church or the ideological support of a dogma" (p. 418). In other words, in a social system which has substituted success for moral obligation or for anything transcending personal well-being and social recognition, the school has become, as a highly specialized plant, the generator of standardized human beings. The parents, having abdicated their responsibility to define aims, are subservient to the system. As the authors again phrase it: "They [the parents] are now viewed by the school somewhat as junior partners in the business of preparing children for material success in temporal life" (p. 284). The children, "so Jung and already Freudened," are caught among contradictory objectives. They are confidently expected to realize all the features which are essential to the pragmatic success-system of the milieu: "humanitarianism, material success, high social status, competition [without showing it], co-operation" (p. 282).

I know that there are in this country, as well as in the country of Horatio Alger and John Dewey, hundreds and thousands of individuals who react against these standardized forces at play around us and upon us. They feel that there are, somewhere, beyond and above mere adjustment to others, values which can give meaning to one's life, that life as it is is not necessarily life as it should be. But the dominating trend on our continent towards automation and conformism means that our lives are being taken away from us. We are becoming fossils in a land of plenty which is also a moral vacuum.

II. OUR DUAL SELF

HOWEVER much these traits characterize us, they do not entirely account for the full, complex Canadian image. There are, mixed with them, deep in us, other identification marks which are inescapably ours and to which we consciously or unconsciously refer when we think of ourselves as different from others. The basic fact about Canada is that our society is not one but two. All Canadians may not agree with this view. But it is irrepressibly held by one half of the nation, and this fact cannot be put aside lightly. Our nation is made of two peoples, the English-speaking and the French-speaking. Even though both have participated in common experiences, have given allegiance to a few similar symbols, and are held together by the same political structure, each has its own sense of identity, its characteristic norms and motivations—in a word, its own culture.

Through the writers' view

Evidences of the differences between the two Canadian societies are found in their respective literatures. If one compares the English and the French literatures in Canada, one discovers that the former expresses itself along an axis which I would see as horizontal while the latter has a more vertical axis. Most critics of English-Canadian literature recognize that one of its essential themes is the tension between man and his milieu, geographical and social. The main characteristic of contemporary novels, since Grove and Callaghan, has been, to use Claude Bissell's words, "contemplative realism." The novel as an art form "should strive to present a tragic vision of man in a realistic social environment."[1] The English-Canadian novel dramatizes as significant human situations where there exists a gap between collective norms and individual behaviour. When the novel is not strictly descriptive, it is implicitly or explicitly moralizing. Or it entwines a political thesis, the defence of a conventional ideal with the frustrations of a human adventure, as in Hugh MacLennan. Or, it depicts the tensions created, in the course of a happy human life, by the blind forces of nature, as in Grove. Or, finally, it depicts the tensions and conflicts between ethnic groups, as in Gwethalyn Graham's *Earth and High Heaven* or John Marlyn's *Under the Ribs of Death*. For most English-Canadian novelists, the novel as artistic expression is more the description and analysis of a social situation than a plunging into the depths of an individual soul. Similarly, the most notable works written for the theatre, for the last fifteen or twenty years, have unceasingly perpetuated, with a new verve and a new gusto, the great tradition of the nineteenth-century English-Canadian theatre, satire. Whether in the plays of Lister Sinclair or of Robertson Davies or of half a dozen other highly talented playwrights, the dominating objective is to uncover and ridicule conformisms, inferiority complexes, and pharisaisms.

What accounts for such a preoccupation in the novel and in the theatre? Must it be related to the geographical scattering of the population? To regional particularisms?

[1]Claude Bissell, "The Novel," *The Arts in Canada*, ed. by Malcolm Ross (Toronto: Macmillan, 1958), p. 93.

To a puritanical tradition? To a religious mentality which is more social or political in interest than supernatural? The beginning of an answer seems to be suggested by the fact that the only non-French Canadian novelists whose works have a vertical dimension, for example, A. M. Klein (*The Second Scroll*) and Adele Wiseman (*The Sacrifice*), are of Jewish origin. Of all the English-speaking Canadians, the person of Jewish ancestry is the one whose cultural heritage is the richer. He is deeply rooted in it, both in Canada and abroad. Whether he accepts it or not, he feels bound to a fate, the beginning and the end of which are given from above and against which he must, like Jacob against the Angel, fight alone. The novels of Mordecai Richler similarly could have been written by contemporary young French-Canadian novelists.

In the writings of these young French-Canadian novelists, as in those of their immediate predecessors, one finds the vertical dimension of which I have been speaking. In the French-Canadian novel, with Langevin, Elie, or Charbonneau, the characteristic tension is one between man and himself. More exactly, it is a tension between the individual and his destiny. Indeed, the central characters of these novels have to fight against their social environment. They are generally introspective young men, shaped by a small and closed society which chokes them with verbalized moral imperatives. They are burnt by unquenchable thirsts. They feel alienated. They live painfully in solitude, tortured by a quasi-metaphysical anguish, in quest of a liberating truth. They are torn between the wish to abdicate and the wish to escape. They are not far from resembling the heroes of James Joyce's *Dubliners*, baffled and entrapped. But the typical drama of the hero of the French-Canadian novel is beyond mere moralizing. Its main drive is towards an Absolute which the hero knows he cannot, in the end, escape. The avenues towards this absolute may be hope, or purity of life, or holiness. He can discard his society: he knows that he cannot discard the tragic freedom of asking who is God and how to reach Him. This direction is equally true of the most vivid plays of the recent French-Canadian theatre, as in the works of Marcel Dubé and Gratien Gélinas. Although the satirical vein is strong in Gélinas' theatre, it is ambiguously carried by an undercurrent of sadness, frustration, and remorse. The plays of more recent playwrights for the theatre or for television, while they dramatize and transpose the contradictions and evils of the local society, also aim at the same basic interrogations of the individual concerning man's fate and man's hope. The institutional stereotypes of the Church and of conventional family life have set in motion strong impulses towards protest and anger. The ultimate, essential truths on which these stereotypes were based and which they have since distorted are deeply ingrained in the individual. It is up to him to re-discover them and to understand them for himself.

Through personal experience

I should like, one day, to collect autobiographies from Canadians, English and French, who have had a sufficient experience of one sort or another with individuals or groups on the other side of the cultural barrier. I would ask them to relate candidly what it has meant for them to enter into communication and co-operation with "the others." We already have some documents of this sort in the published biographies and journals of a few Canadian political figures. But these tell a story at the level of formal and conventional gestures. The personal histories I have in mind would be of a more intimate, direct character. They would point out the typical situations in which French and English encounter one another in our country. They would describe the preconceptions which they have about one another. They would state under what conditions *a priori* notions can be rectified, or maintained and even amplified. They would also bring to the fore the factors which are more potent towards facilitating non-equivocal understanding. They would, in short, throw an unexpected yet necessary light on the predicaments involved in being a Canadian. Presumptuous as this may be, I intend now to venture myself on this delicate path. My own experience may be identical with that of many others. It may be unique. I do not know. I recapitulate it briefly as the adventure of one man of my generation and of my milieu.

I was born in Quebec City where non-French people were and still are so few in number and geographically and socially concentrated in such a self-segregated minority that one could, as I did, spend all one's younger and later years without even noticing them. My earliest, blurred recollection of reference to "les Anglais" is associated with the teaching of Canadian history at the parochial school. The English were to be hated for the "déportation des Acadiens." The real heroes of the Seven Years' War were the French. Montcalm and Lévis overshadowed the touching image of the valiant, poetic Wolfe. The English régime climaxed in the "révolte des patriotes de 1837–8." From this event, we shifted to a colourless Confederation era in which neither teachers nor pupils were interested. Canada essentially meant to me the St. Lawrence area east of Montreal. Almost daily, from spring till late fall, my family would drive a few miles north of Quebec City to my paternal grandfather's farm, which had been in the family's hands for over six generations. It had been "our" land, since the time our ancestor from Saintonge had come here, in 1687, with the regiment of one Chevalier de Saint-Jean. The real "Anglais" in my early life were the "Irlandais." A certain number of Irish families lived in our part of the city and were looked at askance as an alien, aggressive species. The stereotype was reinforced by the almost daily sight of stone fights between Irish children and my schoolmates on our way back from school. For some years—up until 1930—my family spent a few weeks' vacation at a New England seaside resort where I discovered certain amenities of American civilization, enfolded within the protective shield of other French-Canadian families from Montreal and Quebec.

In my adolescent years, I went to college in Montreal. I realized there that the whole of the province of Quebec was not French and that what was strong and dominant in Canada was English. I saw the two cities within the city. The two parts of Ste Catherine Street ran through them, the ugly eastern part through the French district, the attractive western part through the area of English department stores, cinemas, and hotels. I could observe the then expanding well-to-do French suburb of Outremont, but I also noticed the still more impressive area of high social altitude, one I would later know, through Hugh MacLennan, as the "Square Mile." The little jingle of Canadian history which I had learned at the primary school was orchestrated, at college, into a Beethoven-like, devastating concerto in which the French soloists were the admirable protagonists in a duel against endlessly renewed English furies. The heroes of my history of Canada then were Papineau, Chénier, Mercier, Bourassa.

The 24th of May was celebrated as "le jour de Dollard," not as Victoria Day. The writings of the Abbé Groulx were the stock-in-trade for our rhetorical essays. I had a fairly good geographical idea of my country. I had no idea whatsoever of what life was like outside Quebec. The "English-Canadians" were the descendants of those who had crushed the Papineau rebellion, had hanged Riel, had approved the Canadian participation in the Boer War, and had imposed conscription in 1917.

It was only later, when I was a university student, during the late mid-thirties, that I had my first real contacts with English-speaking Canadians. I had then just discovered Canada, through books, at a time when this country existed less than ever. This was the time when the Rowell-Sirois Commission was plotting the causes of national economic frailty on a map from Vancouver to Halifax while thousands of jobless were fleeing hunger on transcontinental box-cars. (Actually, of course, I learned most about these events much later, in literary works as recent as Earle Birney's *Down the Long Table* —as I learnt much of what I now often assume to have known much earlier.) When I first met students from the universities of McGill, Toronto, and Manitoba, around 1936, I realized that the depression era had left on them the same imprint as it had on me. They were of rural or urban middle-class families, as I was. Most of them were members of the Student Christian Movement. Many were later (so I heard) to join the C.C.F. party or to sympathize with political movements or fancies farther left-of-centre. I was a member of no movement. Very much to the contrary. Either because of temperament or because, as a boarder for over six years at college, I had been bored to death by zealous leaders who kept soliciting us into one or the other of the youth movements which pretended to save the world but who amounted only to sonorous prophets of the status quo, I wanted to be left alone. I had no more inclination towards any of the few Quebec semi-nationalist youth associations. Still less, towards the fascist-oriented groupings which bloomed during the period. The preoccupations of many of us were philosophical and aesthetic rather than political.

Yet I was interested in national students' organizations. It was among these groups that I discovered new Canadian friends. Some of them were radicals. Others pretended to be bohemians. They all looked animated by a contagious zeal. And they were, so it seemed to me, at war with, or being emancipated from, the middle-class values of their still puritanical society. Some of my French-Canadian friends and I looked exotic to them. They had read Horace Miner's *Saint-Denis* and they would question us on the family system and the operations of the clergy in Quebec. We discovered that some of the authors we had read and who had influenced us were the same: Silone, Maritain, Malraux. We took the same, republican, side in the Spanish War, and the great preoccupations which crystallized our conversations and our options were of non-Canadian origin. These were of an international, at least European character, and they all more or less centred around the struggle between freedom and the various forms of fascism. But our discussions always remained exclusively political and social. Never was religion a topic of conversation nor did we even venture so far as to refer to spiritual values. There existed between us a feeling of parallelism without real, deep communication.

It was only later, in 1948, when reading *The Pickersgill Letters*,[1] that I discovered, through the intimate cor-

[1]Toronto: Ryerson, 1948.

respondence of at least one young English-Canadian of my generation, that the philosophical and moral questions which were almost the obsession of my French-Canadian friends had also tormented, without our knowing it, some of our English-speaking compatriots of the same generation. The metaphysical and religious explorations of Frank Pickersgill while he was a Toronto student are not dissimilar to those found in the Journal of one of his French-Canadian contemporaries, the poet Saint-Denys Garneau—who, strangely enough, was also to disappear dramatically after having been the silent witness of his own generation. Frank Pickersgill had never met a French Canadian in Canada. When he went to France for postgraduate studies in 1938, the spiritual kinship he felt for that country was idenitcal to the love affair which any French Canadian has with Paris the first time he gets there, indeed even before he reaches it. He knew his Maritain as well as we did. The way he speaks of Bernanos, Mauriac, and Sartre has a more than familiar tone to a French-Canadian ear. He sensed the outstanding value of the review *Esprit* and his cutting comments on true democracy seem to echo the intensely opinionated discussions which we had in Quebec through these pre-war years. As happened to many of us, either at that time or later in our lives, his view of Canada changed while he was abroad. He soon abandoned his native parochialism and he became a more critical judge of our artificial country. Why had we not known Frank Pickersgill? Why had we not identified the Frank Pickersgills in our English-speaking friends of the S.C.M. days? Why had he, why had they not known *La Relève* which had voiced, in anguished terms, the perplexities of our generation and had proclaimed that our predicament resulted not so much from the strait-jackets of a conformist society or from the temporary, erratic determinism of economic forces, but had spiritual dimensions? Why? . . . Perhaps we encountered, and passed, dozens, hundreds of them. Such was the thickness of silence, such was the psychological distance between us, English- and French-speaking Canadians, that we never came to know one another.

Later, at the beginning of my academic career—we were then in the immediate post-war years—I participated resolutely and enthusiastically in the undertakings of such national organizations as the Canadian Youth Commission, the Canadian Citizenship Council, and in adult education experiments. Again, I met men from all across the country, many of whom were my elders, some my contemporaries, all animated with an undaunted zeal for civic and welfare causes. We were a few French-speaking participants not only in the gatherings but in the sharing of the work load. We knew that what we were doing was far beyond the conventional gestures of emotional "bonne entente." There was equal dedication and critical exchange of opinions. The co-operative purpose now was not political but educational. There was, on each side, the assumption and the evidence of moral motivation, but the foundations of co-operation were implicit rather than explicit. Never were the postulates from which each side derived its impulses formulated, nor were the respective patterns of action questioned. Yet how strange it seemed to our nucleus of French-Canadian participants in these undertakings, not so much to hear our English-speaking colleagues refer to such concepts as "democratic spirit," or "the sense of citizenship," or "social welfare," as to see their joyful conviction that, by the mere evangelical use of these concepts, they would magically mobilize hundreds, thousands of their compatriots throughout the country. Such assurance resting on the manipulation of such symbols was utterly alien to our mentality and to our own experience. We knew how hard it was, in our milieu, to mobilize people already so strongly integrated in traditional religious or professional units of social life, and how complex a task it would be to transpose the concepts of citizenship and democratic drive into easily understandable and meaningful terms. Similarly, while our English colleagues in adult education would centre their discussions and efforts on techniques and methods of group work, we would be preoccupied with objectives and the philosophy of group action. Not a few times did we have the feeling that whereas there was formal agreement in our discussions, what went on was a dialogue between deaf men. The big stone which the English-speaking Sisyphus was magnanimously rolling up on one side of the mountain would soon after run down on the other, French, slope of it.

My main association, of course, has been with colleagues in the academic world. There, as could be expected, is the area where one finds the fewest barriers to communication. Either at the annual meetings of the "learned societies" or through participation in national committees or councils, I have experienced the directness of mature relationships. The assumption of frankness is at its maximum and there is, on each side, an expectation of similar scientific objectivity, the reassuring feeling of identical intellectual perspectives. Yet the exchange occurs within an intellectual, often hyper-intellectualized universe of discourse. The rest is taken for granted. The knowledge of French-Canadian society by English-speaking academic colleagues is generally limited to the boundaries of one's professional field. Historians are, of course, the best informed, but their understanding bears on the past; economists, psychologists, geographers, or sociologists may have an accurate knowledge of important aspects of the present, but they often, conversely, lack the historical perspective which would help them to interpret the broader philosophy of life and to understand recent reformulations of it. The interest is global but in some areas remains rather an intention than an achievement. There are outstanding exceptions who, because they know French or for reasons of geography, vocation, or avocation, can be said to participate truly in the two cultures. But it is only recently, in my experience, that conversations with English-speaking friends have reached below the surface, down to the deeper layers where lie the questions which one asks oneself concerning the meaning of one's relations with the rest of the world and with what is beyond it.

Identification and values

What are, then, the ingredients of the value-system, of the sense of identification which characterizes each of the two cultural universes constituting the Canadian nation? This soul-searching has been tried more than once. Will it be useless to try it once more?

Turning first to French-Canadian culture, which I have experienced from the inside, I feel that it is increasingly difficult to generalize about it. At the celebration of the fiftieth anniversary of *Le Devoir*, on January 31, 1960, Gérard Pelletier aptly remarked that instead of talking about the present face of French-Canadian society, one should use the plural and refer to its numerous, contrasting faces. Not only are new socio-economic classes emerging, such as the working class, a bourgeois class of businessmen and entrepreneurs, an intellectual élite more and more aloof from the local society, but each of these is adopting a particular outlook, a specific symbolism, and new attitudes.

Whatever may be these recent internal differentiations, there remains a cultural entity which can be called a French-Canadian "in-group." To be French Canadian means not only to claim a French origin, to speak the French language, to be Catholic in faith, and to share certain traditions. It means basically to identify oneself with the French community in Canada. This identification itself is made through a reference to the same history, which is the history of the French in North America. The sense of history shared by French Canadians is retrospective and nostalgic. One must not forget that the motto of the province of Quebec is "Je me souviens"—I remember. What a French Canadian chiefly remembers is a French paradise lost, as well as the political struggles which, after the British conquest up to the last third of the nineteenth century, conditioned and strengthened his survival. Survival has been the key concept of French-Canadian history-writing and it remains the chief psychological preoccupation of a society set in a culturally and linguistically different continent.

Correspondingly, although the term "French Canada" refers to all the geographical areas in the country where there are numerically important and socially visible groups of French-speaking people, it refers chiefly to the province of Quebec. That province, for French Canadians, is not interchangeable with others. They strongly feel that it is theirs. It is, in a way, what they still hold of the former estate of their ancestors. It is both the framework and the political incarnation of their survival as a cultural group. Canada, for them, is, first of all, Quebec. This historical attitude of self-centredness remains politically dominant, although it has been considerably altered by the professional contacts and allegiances of many groups or classes with their counterparts in the rest of the country. One of the present dilemmas of French-Canadian society is to reconcile its political imperatives, which are centripetal to Quebec, with the dynamic imperatives of its culture which lead to the creation of new institutions and to communication over any sort of boundary. Such cultural communication, of course, is primarily oriented towards France, but modern France has long ceased to be referred to as a mother-country. The chief sources of inspiration of contemporary French-Canadian art and literature are truly indigenous. Academic research and teaching do not follow any particular European pattern. They are spontaneous and try to be authentic. There is an increasing consciousness among those who perform such activities that French Canada is at a cultural cross-roads, that it has now a stimulating incentive to re-define its traditional values and to create new channels of relationships with the broad world.

Because of his long association with, and permeation by the Church, a French Canadian still shows a relatively acute sense of authority which has been emphasized by the traditional family system and by the educational structure. Religion and language are bound in an immemorial association and the humanistic education of the classical colleges has perpetuated an intellectual tradition which gives priority to ideas over techniques, to moral obligations over empirical experience. It is a truism to repeat that a French Canadian does not think of democracy in the same way as his English-speaking compatriot. Traditionally encouraged by a paternalistic Church to submit to political rulers and to accept the established social order, he does not have the feeling that the government is his government. It may be less true today than it was fifty years ago to say that he is a faithful parishioner more than an active citizen. On the whole, he remains more an electoral than a truly political being.

My perception of the culture of the English-speaking Canadian world, from the outside, is bookish, vicarious, and fragmentary. So is it also, I fancy, for many English-speaking Canadians themselves. I know that this social world is far from homogeneous. Long before I could personally observe its regional diversity, I had read that it was a mosaic. I had also read, in the works of many observers from André Siegfried to Mason Wade, that within the mosaic there was a consistent design. Notwithstanding the provincial differences, the traditions of numerous lively ethnic groups, the economic stratification, and the religious compartments, certain unmistakable traits distinguish the *homo canadensis* from any other.

One of the traits of the English-speaking Canadian, as I see it, cannot be described easily. It has something to do with living in a country which is too large, unhumanized, and too thinly populated. I would call it an identification through a sense of geographical and social void. To be Canadian is to be involved in this reference to emptiness and drabness. What other feeling can one have in a country, as Northrop Frye has described it, "divided by . . . great stretches of wilderness, so that its frontier is a circumference rather than a boundary; a country with huge rivers and islands that most of its natives have never seen; a country that has made a nation out of the stops on two of the world's longest railway lines . . .?"[1] In such a wide and wild country, how can one's allegiance extend

---

[1] "Preface to an Uncollected Anthology," in *Studia Varia*, Royal Society of Canada, Literary and Scientific papers, ed. by E. G. D. Murray, F.R.S.C. (Toronto: University of Toronto Press, 1957), p. 21.

to the whole of it? Allegiance here is more like that of the solitary for his solitude. At the most, it can be given to one's local community or to one's region. On the other hand, this aptitude for withdrawing is fortunately paralleled and counteracted by a feeling of pride in participation in the technological conquest of man over an alien nature. Being Canadian also means having reduced the handicaps created by the Laurentian Shield. "The ninety years of [Canada's] nationhood," writes C. B. Macpherson, "have been dominated by two endeavours . . . expansion and survival."[1] The satisfaction derived from survival in an inhuman environment and from economic expansion against a constantly challenging frontier creates strong bonds of attachment which, brutal as they may be, are deeply possessive.

Thus it seems that the interest of Canadians in their country, basically, is as much economic as it is political. The "North Americanism which is Canadian and not 'American,' " to which Malcolm Ross refers,[2] is also a result of a gradual attainment of political autonomy within the British Commonwealth of Nations. English-speaking Canadians are emotionally attached to a relatively recent Canada which has emancipated itself from colonialism and which has consequently and currently differentiated itself from the United States. Although there exists a "latent loyalty" to the British throne and to the Crown as symbol, the manifest allegiance to our own country has been crystallized by the participation in two world wars for the defence of it. It has often been when they were abroad, away from their country, either in war or in peace, that Canadians have discovered it for the first

[1] C. B. Macpherson, "The Social Sciences," in *The Culture of Contemporary Canada*, ed. by Julian Park (Ithaca, N.Y.: Cornell University Press, 1957), p. 181.
[2] Malcolm Ross, Introduction to *Our Sense of Identity*, p. ix.

time. They have then also discovered, almost with surprise, that they were proud of it.

At the core of the Canadian pride lies a quasi-religious belief in democratic government, more precisely, in British parliamentary institutions. Democracy is the overall concept which comprises not only a political credo in individual freedom, a transcendental faith in the individual, but a whole way of life. This way of life invites co-operation with one's neighbours and it is tolerant. Tolerance is also a religious attitude and it involves the recognition of any variety of religion. Religion is left to the individual's choice, but it may lend itself, in situations of collective frustration or crisis, to movements of social protest and to reformist political action.

This over-simplification may not correspond to the real experience of what it is to be an English Canadian. Again, it is the view of it which one has from the outside. Fortunately, there have been, in recent years, more and more English- and French-speaking Canadians who have had a common experience of co-operation and of closer acquaintance with one another, in public administration and political life, in academic and scientific circles, in professional associations, in business and labour organizations, in welfare and artistic national councils of various sorts. The process still seems hesitant. It is only recently that an English-Canadian writer, Hugh MacLennan, in *Two Solitudes*, has become aware of the dramatic dimensions of Canadian co-existence. It was a French-Canadian novelist, Jean Simard, who, to my knowledge, was the first among Canadian writers with enough intuition, knowledge, and audacity to create a character belonging to the "other" cultural world.[1]

[1]In his novel *Les sentiers de la nuit* (Montréal: Le Cercle du Livre de France, 1959).

III. OUR COMMON
INTELLECTUAL HERITAGE

THE rapprochement between French- and English-speaking Canada has been particularly visible in the academic world. Canadian intellectuals have become more aware of their respective spiritual heritages. They now see more clearly the similarities between these. They are more and more conscious of the fact that, beneath the institutional and psychological differences in thought-orientation, in curriculum, and in pedagogical methods within each culture, there are historical sources which are common to both. If we are ambitious to define the dynamic objectives of concerted action, we must reach for this solid foundation of our intellectual life. Both the French and English intellectual traditions in Canada have flowered out of classical humanism. To recapture the meaning of the spiritual community from which humanism developed and to ascertain some of its subsequent acquisitions may be one of the most fruitful ways of finding our common denominator.

In a recent essay, on *Philosophy in the Mass Age,* George Grant, following Santayana, has recalled the differences between the humanism which arose out of the Catholic tradition and that which arose in a Protestant climate.[1] Whatever these historical differences may have

[1]George Grant, *Philosophy in the Mass Age* (Toronto: Copp Clark, 1959), ch. VII.

been, they should not obscure the fact that both derived from the same mediaeval source. They have their still more ancient source in the Graeco-Roman Mediterranean tradition. This theme was strongly elaborated in one of the most stimulating briefs submitted to the Massey Commission in 1950 by the Institute of Mediaeval Studies of the University of Montreal.[1] Mediaeval culture, this brief recalls, was a moment of tremendous spiritual density. It integrated not only the letter but the spirit of antiquity. It introduced to the Western conscience the *Nicomachean Ethics* and the moral ideal which was at its core. It created the "university." By assimilating and enhancing Aristotle, it assimilated the best of Hellenism and rejuvenated man's thinking. It was through it that classical humanism recaptured the sense of human excellence which had been formulated by the Greek and the Roman civilizations.

Two typical intellectual trends, in contrast and often in opposition to each other, had characterized ancient thought. One, isocratic or sophistic, aimed at the education of the ideal man of action and emphasized the priority of the arts of language. It culminated in rhetoric and it found its most complete expression in Cicero's *De oratore*. The other trend, platonic and aristotelian, favoured science and speculation. Both trends remained harmoniously interwoven in the Middle Ages but the Renaissance created a divorce which Western thought has perpetuated, often painfully, down to the present time: that between "humanities" and the "sciences."

The humanists of the Renaissance emphasized the Greek and the Roman ideal types of men as permanently

---

[1]This brief is substantially reported in: Thomas-André Audet o.p., "Etudes médiévales et culture canadienne," *Revue Dominicaine*, LVI (février 1950), 66–79.

exemplary ideals, yet they somewhat forgot concurrent Greek and Roman traditions of scientific inquiry. They were curious about the literary, aesthetic, and philosophical achievements of antiquity, but less curious about its social and political institutions, as indeed they were about their own. Their classical humanism remained chiefly literary and philosophical, dissociated from scientific inquiry into the nature of the physical world and of the social world. Yet the other intellectual current sprung from antiquity, that of systematic curiosity and experimentation, developed brilliantly on its own momentum, thanks to men like Bacon and Da Vinci, later Descartes and Pascal. It was, however, concentrated on the physical world. Scientific investigation was concerned with what was non-human and outside of man, not with what man was as an individual and as a social being. Consequently, when the teaching of humanities, in the eighteenth century, partly annexed the teaching of sciences, these were still only "natural" or "physical" sciences.

It was only much later that, capitalizing on the wealth of ethnographic material accumulated by the world discoverers and historians, as well as on the new vistas opened by the Enlightenment's philosophers and the French encyclopaedists, the social sciences developed, at the beginning of the nineteenth century. The history of their eventual differentiation one from another and of the elucidation of their methodology is a colourful, often painful history up until after the beginning of the present century. That history can be best described by Paul Valéry's observation: "Dans le passé, on n'avait guère vu, en fait de nouveautés, paraître que des solutions ou des réponses à des problèmes ou à des questions très anciennes, sinon immémoriales. Mais notre nouveauté, à nous, consiste dans l'inédit des questions elles-mêmes, et non point des solutions; dans les énoncés, et non dans les réponses."[1]

The social sciences have formulated these new problems posed for modern men by the industrial age and changing societies. They are both the expression of a social challenge and the response to that challenge. Each in its own fashion—economics, political science, sociology or any other of them—has enabled us to decipher the network of social determinisms within which man's fate is being lived. They help us to ascertain the objective reality of man as a social being. In so doing, they have widened our conception of man and they oblige us to widen also the traditional concept of humanism. Sociology and social anthropology, in particular, by uncovering the multiplicity of human cultures, have pushed back the frontiers within which one formerly looked for a stable, uni-directional definition of human nature. The social sciences have brought about a de-Westernization of the concept of culture and of civilization. Henceforth, "à une conception du peuple élu, de la nation souveraine, de la civilisation dominante, de l'individu privilégié, a succédé un schéma global où figurent sur le même plan, pris dans la même histoire, réagissant les uns sur les autres avec les mêmes droits et la même dignité, toutes les cultures et tous les hommes."[2]

Thus, to the traditional meaning of culture, understood as the intellectual development of the individual apt to appreciate "the finer things of life" in Western society, has been added a wider sociological concept according to which culture is defined as "the total way of life of any society." In so far as the social sciences endeavour,

[1]Paul Valéry, "Bilan de intelligence," in *Variété III* (Paris: Gallimard, 1936), p. 276.
[2]Jean d'Ormesson, Introduction to "Condition de l'homme," *La Nef*, Paris, 13e année, Cahier no 13, Nouvelle série, juin 1956, p. 14.

each pursuing its particular query, to identify and to comprehend, from society to society, the constancy and recurrence of cultural conditions which fashion the personality and the life-orientation of human individuals, they constitute a vast problematical investigation of man.

Such is, or should be, the perspective of modern humanism. Without discarding the sense of a hierarchy of values in man or the sense of the excellence of man's spiritual achievements which characterized the traditional humanism, it must add a sense of the pluralism which the forms of man's excellence can show. Such a widened humanism is never definitely "given." It consists in a long, patient, and systematic investigation, an investigation corresponding to the need which modern man has of becoming conscious of himself.

IV. THE NEW HUMANISM: A CHALLENGE

I T is in our universities that the latent humanistic values of Canadian life can be re-evaluated and incarnated. Canada will achieve sooner and more powerfully the fusion of its dual cultural heritages by intellectual avenues rather than political. And there can be such an achievement in our institutions of higher learning if we bring forth, with imagination and conviction, the creative potentialities of classical humanism, rejuvenated by the broad perspectives of the social sciences.

This is the great challenge, as I see it, to which Canadians must repond if we are to become true to our deep, real selves, and if we are to make a contribution to the world in which we live. It is in its institutions of higher learning that the guiding light of a nation must originate. This light, in our country, will, to a great extent, result from the integration of the permanent and lasting acquisitions of the old world with the discoveries of the modern one. The North American world around us is a Pandora's box of titanic proportions. What it has to offer and what we have already borrowed from it is far from all evil. It contains latent ambitions and nostalgias for the ideal, and it is animated by an adventurous spirit. It has made fascinating explorations of the nature of man's mind and of man's behaviour as a social animal. We in Canada must make ours a similarly bold spirit with the aim of assuming a positive responsibility in the leadership of Western civilization.

If we are to do this, our universities must take up again a conviction that they are, essentially and above all, *republics of learning*. They should re-discover the true meaning of the "university," an institution shaped by the Middle Ages as the pedagogical embodiment of its own intellectual integration. I am not advocating a return to the past, as past, but suggesting an example of innovation through recourse to a dynamic model. In order to create our own model, we must resist the forces which would make our universities mere factories for the production of technicians or large-scale cafeterias catering to the whims and fancies of a flighty public. We must re-habilitate the notion that education and learning are valuable ends in themselves. We should revive the ancient concept of the *Magister* who was a seeker of truth and a lover of wisdom. Education, as it has been said, is an act of self-discovery and a judgment upon the self thus discovered—by it a man re-discovers the past, grasps the most profound and hidden currents of the present, and thereby comes to know himself in depth as well as in breadth.

If the university wishes to become again a true republic of learning, it must not only make possible but stimulate what, according to Plato, is the true form of human thought: the dialogue. First, the dialogue between masters of varied humanistic and scientific disciplines. Also, the widened dialogue between masters and students. This means that the one who teaches will have to remain, as was the Scholar in the old sense of the term, an "inner-directed" or a "tradition-directed" person. What he must communicate is a super-abundance of his own, personal research. In order to be able to do this, he must be allowed every possible opportunity—financial, administrative, and academic— of dedication to his subject and to his students; that is, to contemplation and communication.

If Canadian universities can carry out this role in a more explicit and a more original way than ever, I am convinced that all the other important things which we are looking for shall be added unto us. We shall, as Jacques Barzun said, "keep the men who run our national educational plant from being run by it." Running it with their minds set on a re-discovery of what gives meaning and consistentcy to the lives of men, they will provide the community with a more powerful anchor.

V. THE SOCIAL SCIENCES
IN CANADA

T H E social sciences have broadened the traditional humanism. They are a challenge to higher education in our country in so far as they stimulate us to reconcile the acquisitions of the classical tradition with the values of the new world. Let us consider this challenge further and see how the social sciences offer us a tool for a better definition of our nation as well as for a better definition of our international relations in a smaller and smaller, more and more complex world.

The establishment of the social sciences in Canada is a fairly recent event. They are not older than forty years or so. As C. B. Macpherson has shown, their development has reproduced the two main endeavours which have dominated Canada's accession to nationhood: "The patterns of social and historical thought in Canada, their rates and directions of growth, have been shaped in various ways by the two impulsions of expansion and survival, which in a sense, contain each other."[1] As the economic, political, and social problems created by Canada's expansion broke out with sufficient magnitude, particularly at the turn of the century, they had to be settled by the politicians. But, as Macpherson also notes,

[1]C. B. Macpherson, in *The Culture of Contemporary Canada*, p. 181.

"It gradually became realized, perhaps from the fact that the politicians could never get the problems settled, that the cultivation of some specifically Canadian social sciences would be advantageous." Individual scholars and groups of scholars in the fields of economics, history, and political science appeared in Canadian universities and were "the main authors of the social and historical writing of our time."[1]

The social sciences in Canada, then, have appeared as a response to the challenge of the environment, both physical and social, and they have, in their turn, brought about changes in this environment. This process of counter-play could be illustrated in the fields of geography, demography, ethnology, and anthropology, as well as economics, political science, and sociology. One has only to recall such monumental studies as W. A. Mackintosh's "Canadian Frontiers of Settlement" series; C. A. Dawson's "Peace River Settlement" series; the late H. A. Innis's classic monographs on the economics of the fish, lumber, fur, and railroad industries; "Canadian Government Series," first edited by the late R. MacGregor Dawson—not to mention the equally imposing works of the historians and of the anthropologists.

The development of social sciences in French Canada has similarly reflected for the last twenty-five years or so the processes of the milieu in which they were born. The impact there was accelerated by industrialization and by the de-structuration of a formerly homogeneous society. Social sciences were the tool by which could be described the changes in values, the social implications of these changes, and their repercussions. They were also a tool for a re-definition of the community's objectives and of the new forms of its communication with others.

[1]*Ibid.*, p. 182.

As they progressed along different paths, often on intersecting or diverging avenues, the social scientists felt the need for a rationalization of their efforts—which itself might help focus their respective objectives and even co-ordinate them. This need was fulfilled with the creation, in 1938, of the Social Science Research Council, which has been, ever since, an invaluable superstructure in Canadian academic life. It has not only fostered interest in and encouragement of the social sciences, inside and outside the universities. It has made possible, too, co-operation between the social scientists and the humanists, through an intimate relationship with the Humanities Research Council which was also created in 1945. Thanks to this alliance, many collective projects in social research have been undertaken by the Council on problems which had vital significance in contemporary Canadian social life. Thanks to such research, we have acquired a truer and more objective portrait of ourselves.

It is through the experience gained by personal association with one of these projects that I want to submit some further thoughts on the nature of the Canadian nation. This project was chiefly sociological in scope, and its purpose was to study the nature of bi-culturalism in Canada. Many individuals and groups collaborated in it and the result of their observations and efforts has now become manifest in the form of a book of essays on Canadian dualism.[1] What I shall have to say does not involve the opinion of any of the contributors to that volume. I merely want to formulate some elements of a sort of sociological model in the perspective of which

[1]*Canadian Dualism: Studies of French-English Relations / La Dualité canadienne: Essais sur les relations entre Canadiens français et Canadiens anglais*, ed. by Mason Wade (University of Toronto Press; Presses Universitaires Laval, 1960), 427 pp.

I have tried to give meaning to the work of my colleagues and to my own perception of Canada. Our country has always been in quest of its identity. My present effort is added to countless others which have been made, in the past, to reach a clearer view of what we are and why we are what we are.

VI. A MODEL FOR THE UNDERSTANDING OF CANADA

T H E model which I suggest takes into account first the elementary fact that Canada is a single federal political structure superimposed transcontinentally almost in contradiction to north-south geographical forces. Our country combines the diversities of at least five natural economic areas. These, in their turn, are carved out into ten provincial political units, each with its Confederation-old tradition of bargaining against the central power, each constituting a strategic framework for the definition of local interests and of self-centred allegiances. Ten provinces, unforgettably portrayed in A. M. Klein's ironical poem:

> [Ten] of them . . .
> But the heart seeks one, the heart, and also the mind
> seeks single the thing that makes one, if one.
>   Yet where shall one find it? In their history—
> the cairn of cannonball on the public square?
> Their talk, their jealous double-talk? Or in
> The whim and weather of a geography
> curling in drifts about the forty-ninth? . . .
>
>   Or hear it sing
> from the house with towers, from whose towers ring
> bells, and the carillon of laws? . . .

> What
> to name it, that is sought?
> The ladder the [ten] brothers hold by rungs? . . .
>
> Or find it, find it, find it commonplace
> but effective, valid, real, the unity
> in the family feature, the not unsimilar face?[1]

This geographical and provincial diversity provides the backdrop on the stage. The Canadian scene is also animated by numerous groups of various ethnic origins who constitute over one-fifth of the country's population. To them has been added, since the end of World War II, the stimulating flow of immigrants who have sought in our country either a haven or a secure democratic place to live. Many of these groups have kept cherished customs, or the use of their language, or deep allegiances to the memories of their countries of more or less ancient origin. They constitute lively elements of Canadian social pluralism.

Notwithstanding the political unity cementing many social diversities, the dominant fact of Canada as a nation is that it is composed of two major linguistic universes, the English- and the French-speaking. Each of these has its own culture which is itself embodied in the fabric and the structures of a characteristic type of society. These two linguistic and cultural groups have historically constituted the essential partners of national life, almost two nations within the nation. The history of contemporary Canada is the history of the contacts, oppositions, tensions, conflicts and gradual rapprochement between the two. As one of Canada's most brilliant essayists, Malcolm Ross, has written: "We are inescap-

[1]A. M. Klein, "The Provinces," *The Rocking Chair and other Poems* (Toronto: Ryerson Press, 1948), p. 2–3. The poem, of course, says "*Nine* of them." I hope the author will permit my political alteration.

ably, and almost from the first, the bi-focal people."[1] Canada as a political entity is largely the result of adjustment between these cultural universes, between two people whose association has often been referred to as a "mariage de raison." The leading postulate in the perspective by which the interaction and the relationships between these two partners should be perceived is not assimilation but duality. Too often in the past the mistake has been made of considering the fate of the French, in Canada, in the light of the history of minority groups in the United States, as though the two situations were comparable. Modern North America has been settled by immigrants from Europe, Africa, and Asia. As each new group entered, there set in, with varying rapidity, a process known as "americanization." It was assumed generally that the end result would be the same: the almost complete disappearance of the marks of the country from which the immigrants came. Not a few studies on Canada have adopted a similar scheme of interpretation. They have assumed that French Canadians would be gradually assimilated. The French-Canadian people as an entity would or should disappear by being absorbed into the large universe of the English-speaking people. But this view, implying that French Canada is only one among the variety of groups of non-English-speaking origin, and that French Canadians do not differ from any other "minority" group in the United States or in Canada, is contrary to history and sociologically erroneous.[2]

Minorities are of many kinds. At least four specifically different varieties can be distinguished: the status minor-

[1]*Our Sense of Identity*, p. ix.
[2]See Everett C. Hughes, "Regards sur le Québec, *Essais sur le Québec contemporain* (Québec: Les Presses Universitaires Laval, 1953), ch. x.

ity; the diaspora; the immigrant minority; and a fourth category, which Everett Hughes has called the "charter member" minority. French Canadians constitute in Canada a minority of this latter kind. They have become a minority by virtue of invasion, of conquest. They have a deep consciousness of having been in the country first. They are charter members of Canada. Hence their determination to be recognized as having a special claim on it. Hence their conviction, emphasized by a feeling of deep-rootedness, of being different from other minority groups.

This definition of themselves by the French Canadians is accentuated by their conception of the constitution of the country. In the eyes of the French Canadians, the British North America Act which created the Canadian Confederation is not only a juridical act of the Imperial government creating Canadian provinces and binding them into a federal unit. It is also a covenant between the English-speaking majority and the French-speaking cultural minority of the Canadian nation. It is a pact, according to which French-speaking Canadians obtained recognition of their status as partners in the government and in the life of the whole nation.

The characteristic process of English-French relationships has not been one of assimilation but one of progressive differentiation, of cultural duality within the framework of a single national political unit. From this follows the other sociological postulate that Canada must be seen as a social whole constituted of two interacting parts, uneven in size and in density, but from both of which it derives its individuality. Although the whole is greater that the sum of these two parts, to understand Canada will be, first, to understand its two constituting elements, each in itself and for itself, and also in its relationship with the other.

I have previously set forth some specific features of the French and English societies in Canada. Each of the two societies is heterogeneous but each has definite traits which are not interchangeable with those of the other. The boundaries between them are not geographical but linguistic and cultural. Reference to history and to the contemporary situation shows that each one has its own sense of identification, its own concept of history and of its role in the nation. Each has its own philosophy of life, its own notion of religion. Each preserves its own educational system. Each has, even, its own conception of Canada. Each has its preferred national symbolism, its favourite heroes, its different holidays.

But if each of these two individualized elements must be seen and understood in itself and for itself, it is sociologically as important that each should be seen and understood in its relationship with the other. The understanding of inter-group relations must be focused, first of all, on the relation. As Everett Hughes again expresses it, ethnic relations can be no more understood by studying either one or the other, or one and the other, of the groups involved than can a chemical combination, by an analysis of each discrete element, or a boxing bout by successive observation of the two fighters.[1] No matter how different from each other the two Canadian cultural groups are, each has been part with the other of an interacting system, each one must be seen as participant in this play and counter-play and as a result of it. The act of living together and acting upon one another, even in a negative or in an aggressive fashion, transforms the very nature of each participant. The English and the

[1]Everett C. Hughes, "The Study of Ethnic relations," *Dalhousie Review, XXVII* (Jan., 1948), 479.

French societies in Canada are not a product of isolation. Each is a product of interaction with the other. It has been one objective of the book on *Canadian Dualism* to undertake such an analysis. The contributors to these essays endeavoured to establish the extent to which the social institutions, the ideologies, the attitudes of one group had influenced those of the other. How deeply, for example, have the patterns of the life ambitions of the young French Canadians been influenced, in one way or another, by English-Canadian models? What does the French, originally Catholic labour movement in Quebec owe to its relationship with national "English" labour organizations? To what extent has the French language been transformed because of exposure to English? To what extent have thought-patterns and ideologies been transformed? Reciprocally, what has been the impact, if any, on English-speaking Canada, of the French-Canadians' educational system, of their enthusiasm for liberal arts, of their enjoyment of the good life as something not necessarily sinful? Unfortunately, we know very little about all this. The most interesting questions often remain without an answer, although many contributors to this book bring out fascinating observations in the fields of economics, politics, and even religion. One of the areas where reciprocal influence and cross-fertilization were least expected is that of law. Yet Professor Louis Baudoin of McGill University meticulously describes the ways in which French civil law, in the province of Quebec, has been gradually transformed by the influences of the common law, not only in matters of interpretation but, in many cases, of conceptualization. Reciprocally, there seems to have been a counter-influence, on Canadian jurisprudence, of the French philosophy of law and of its need for clarity of definition.

VII. PSYCHOLOGICAL AND POLITICAL CONSEQUENCES

SUCH have been the processes of the Canadian symbiosis. If we were more fully aware of them, there would follow a certain number of important consequences in our national life. First, in our sense of identification with the country. We would see with new conviction that to accept Canada in its wholeness is not so much a spontaneous emotional attitude as an act of reason. Canada is not a starting point but a goal. It is not a datum but a construct. It is a becoming, and there is no definitely set pattern to follow for becoming it. Patterns and objectives have to be constantly redefined and improvised. A well-tempered, yet positive, national life will consist always, as it has in the past, in such a motion. But in a motion which, as Malcolm Ross so vividly described it, will remain founded on tension. "A motion which takes its energy in tension, a motion which is visible in unfolding spirals of irony, a motion in which nothing is left behind or lost."[1]

One such spiral of irony at the moment can be seen in the fact that English-speaking Canadians are undergoing an experience which is not dissimilar to an earlier experience of the French Canadians and which may help them to understand the latter better. More and more of

[1]*Our Sense of Identity*, p. xii.

them are alarmed at seeing what they cherish in their Canadian way of life submitted to certain sterilizing influences of American culture. Seeing their own culture endangered makes it dearer and worth preserving and defending. This produces a feeling of self-identification and cultural assertion which may not be nationalism, as such, but which reflects a determined effort for survival. Now such an effort and such a struggle towards self-recognition has been a long story for French Canada and it has been the root of what was often misleadingly called French-Canadian "nationalism." The French Canadian has had the experience of seeing his culture endangered or compromised by alien forces. For the English Canadian to meditate over this experience and to relate it to his own, might be a fruitful way of discovering an area of psychological *rapprochement* with, and perhaps of forming an attitude of renewed interest in, the French Canadian.

But, whatever the *rapprochement* may be, it will have to rest, it will be all the stronger if it rests, on the recognition of duality. This cultural duality has been, in recent years, stated in eloquent terms in many public documents and, in particular, in the reports of the Massey Commission and of the Fowler Commission. The official definition which our country has given of itself, on many occasions, even in speeches or statements by the Queen, has asserted, even emphasized this duality. *Un-hyphenated canadianism is a fiction.* But this assertion should not be merely verbal or official. It should be recognized with conviction. Its practical consequences must be carried out earnestly at all levels of daily life, in Ottawa as in Quebec; in many other places in Canada as it is in Quebec; on TCA airlines as on railroads. I am not advocating any separatist attitude nor any policy which would, on the part of the provincial government of Quebec, mean a defensive or aggressive attitude towards the central Canadian government as though the capital of the country were the capital of a foreign country. All that I am arguing is that if a bi-cultural country is going to make any headway, it has to take its twinship into account.

Other consequences of the twinship will follow, on the level of internal national policy. I have already referred to the well-known fact that Canada, as we know it, is politically the outcome of constant compromises. It is the result of round-table discussions. Our constitution was elaborated in this way. Our national policy has been shaped and remodelled at the cost of innumerable, often endless, Royal Commissions. We can either deplore this or rejoice in it, but we have actually not much choice. Such a style of national policy-making is inevitable in a country which came into being under the pressure of economic and geographical forces from outside rather than by a collective wish from inside. It is necessary to recall once more that we did not have here a collective national revolution, such as has occurred in most modern nations. We did not have a collective act of political emancipation out of which, as happened for other nations, we might have spontaneously created the symbols identifying and perpetuating our rise to adulthood: a flag, a national anthem, a national holiday. We may regret that we have missed, or been by-passed by, such an occasion. It is too late now for regret.

Our nation has become adult through patience and without colour. It has had the sober beginning of a "mariage de raison" between two partners who did not chose to live together. Consequently, we should not make too much effort to create artificially the symbols of national life which history has refused to us. We should refrain from imposing on ourselves a meaningless national symbolism. A national flag cannot properly be born out of round-table discussions or parliamentary committees. The result—and we already have more than one indication of it—might too easily look like an abstract hooked-rug, designed and woven by blind artists of conflicting schools of painting. We may regret not having that expression of nationhood, but we may discover, in another, higher perspective, that it is a blessing. Perhaps, in a not too distant future, in a world where national boundaries will have become meaningless and national arrogance catastrophic, we may be envied by many other nations as "the country without a flag."

VIII. OUR INTERNATIONAL
RESPONSIBILITY

THE fact of having been by-passed by the extreme forms of nationalism and by nationalism itself, if it seems an apparent weakness domestically, is an element of strength in our international relationships. Canada's international policy and attitude in world affairs have shown distinctive characteristics which draw the attention, often the admiration of an increasing number of nations. Some of these traits are prudence, understanding, tolerance, and an unflinching zeal for peace. These qualities on the international scene reflect and derive from the necessities of our behaviour on the domestic scene. Prudence and understanding have been the conditions of relative peace in a country which had to live on compromise. And that prudence, as Malcolm Ross again puts it, is not a negative virtue: "If it seems to suggest immobility, let us think of the immobility at the centre of a moving wheel."[1] It is prudence which sets us in motion, and in international affairs, that motion has been around a central act of faith in other people's goodwill and reason, in their ability to use these qualities for salvation rather than destruction.

I have a strong feeling that one of the reasons for Canada's growing international prestige is our relative

[1] *Our Sense of Identity*, p. ix.

lack of biases and prejudices in our dealings with others and consequently, our attitude of attention to others and of understanding of their problems. Indeed, we have preferences, within the Western world, which are not exclusively determined by economic or strategic interests. It is normal and immensely valuable, for example, that the texture of our bonds with the countries of the Commonwealth be as strong as it is flexible. But I consider it as profoundly significant that we should have been so alive to the ambitions of the countries of Asia and Africa who have lately attained the status of independence; that we should have been so mindful in recognizing the form of government which they wanted for themselves; and that we should have been so spontaneously ready to help those among them who are in need of economic or technical aid. But I am not the only one to wish that our presence in international affairs and our role in determining global policy should be more positive, even more dynamic. Qualities other than mere prudence will be more and more needed. For prudence often degenerates into, or simply conceals, hesitation or uncertainty. As an optimistic friend of Canada recently expressed it: "It will be one of the problems of Canadian leadership in the next few years to think out Canadian policies that are not simply the policies of the honest broker, but the policies that the great powers do not, for whatever reason, think out or propose. But it will not be enough to propose a policy, it will be necessary to put behind it the weight of an enlightened country."[1]

We are all concerned with our relationship with the world of the hydrogen bomb as well as with our stand

[1]Denis William Brogan, "An Outsider Looking in," in *Canada's Tomorrow*, ed. by G. P. Gilmour (Toronto: Macmillan, 1954), p. 276.

in the alignment of the two great blocks of forces now confronting each other. This struggle, as we know, is most likely to stop short of global destructive war and it has already been reduced to a level of competition which is economic and cultural. In this perspective, we are far from having formulated our policies with enough imagination. We have much more to offer than we have done, so far, to the underdeveloped countries of the "Third World" in Asia and Africa. These countries are technologically less developed than we are and they are culturally developed in a manner different from ours. We have to enter into greater and better communication with them. But in order to communicate with them, we must understand them. We must comprehend more fully what their respective cultures are and what we have to offer to them: the values of our own Western civilization. Before entering into a dialogue with others, we must have a clear view of who we are and who they are. Are we ready to answer such a challenge? I would like, at this point, to refer to some observations made previously and to widen the scope of the challenge which I then offered to institutions of higher learning in our country.

From social anthropology and sociology we have learned the equal importance of the culture of each society and of any type of civilization. This must be the framework of our new outlook. We must de-Westernize our concept of civilization. This will require an effort since we have been trained to confuse our own civilization with Civilization itself. We must become aware that there have been forms of wisdom, ideals of good life, patterns of social structures and of government, such as those of India or China, which are much more ancient than the norms which we value in our civilization. They have not only documentary interest. They are still the meaningful models of life for millions of peoples. Actually, we have no choice either to do this or not to do it, for, in the words of the great Indian scholar, Sardepali Radakrishnan, "the days of cultural tribalism, of separate cultural universes, are over. We belong to the same world. Our tribe is mankind and nothing that is human is alien to us. . . . The new world-environment requires a tradition which is neither Eastern or Western but universal and based on the conception of man, on the recognition of his uniqueness, the freedom and creativity of the individual person, the demand for personal dignity and autonomy."[1]

Such a responsibility does not mean that we have to attenuate, still less to forget, our Western values. On the contrary, for we shall be in a position to enter into fruitful dialogue with other civilizations only in so far as we have a full grasp of all the values of our civilization and of their intellectual, moral, and political implications. As I indicated earlier, the rejuvenation of Canadian intellectual life as well as a better polarization of our general way of life depend on a return to the sources of the Western civilization which we have inherited from Rome, Greece, and Israel. In an address delivered at the annual summer school for teachers at Oxford, in the summer of 1959, on "The Essential Values of Western Civilization," the Honourable Lester B. Pearson summarized these values vividly: "From the Greeks," he said, "we have received the ideal of quality before quantity, of honour before wealth, balance before bigness, principles before practice, and in law, politics and military service, the superiority of the dedicated amateur over the professional. . . . From Rome we have received a tradition of order and

---

[1]Sarvepali Radhakrishnan, Opening address at the Tenth Session of the General Conference of UNESCO, Paris, November 1958.

organization, of one law for all citizens, of the essential personal responsibility of every citizen to do his duty to the state. . . . From Israel came the spiritual heritage of one God, and the worth and value and equal rights of every person under that God." To this richness have been added the treasures of the humanistic tradition, of a democratic ideal, of the scientific method applied to the physical as well as the social world, and of new goals in life created by stupendous technological inventions. We have to reconcile the youth of our human experience and the use of our too rapidly acquired wealth with ancient notions concerning the immediate and ultimate goods of human life. To this challenge which is confronting, above all, our institutions of higher learning, is added the challenge of making our values known to peoples of other civilizations. Our communication with them must be a two-way process, for we may have much to borrow and to learn from them. How fruitfully, for example, could we not refresh our concepts of human rights and of human freedoms by exposing them to the candid vigour of oriental wisdoms which, many centuries before Plato and Aristotle, had formulated an ideal of human peace and deference! How much would we not benefit from re-discovering the sense of harmony and the noble prescriptions of such systems of ethics as those of Confucius, Achoka, or Buddha which, more than many Western ethnical systems, have insisted on the demands of human dignity!

One timely incentive towards this urgent task is provided to us by the ten-year "major project" of Unesco on "the mutual appreciation of Eastern and Western values." Canada is alertly co-operating in this project, through its National Commission for Unesco and through some universities. This is only a beginning, and it points to the right direction. Canada has, on the Pacific, a wide-open window on Asia. In three Canadian universities, McGill, Toronto, and British Columbia, there are research institutes on Asia. These and similar institutes should develop. They should become, along with institutes of mediaeval studies, with faculties of philosophy and letters, and with humanities departments, the most highly treasured laboratories of Canadian universities. We have made fairly satisfactory headway in the technical or professional departments of human learning in the natural and the social sciences. We should now give to ourselves, and to others, the image of a people whose ambition is not so much to reach the moon, as to transcend our psychological space in order to reach the nations around us, closer at hand, but also better worth loving.